LEADERSHIP
INTO THE
21ST CENTURY

Edited by Wetherill Staff

Royersford, Pennsylvania

THE ALPHA PUBLISHING HOUSE

ALPHA PUBLISHING HOUSE
475 North Lewis Road • Royersford, PA 19468

ISBN 1-881074-04-8
Printed in the United States of America

"Of all the vital faculties available to man, the ability to base one's life on the principle of absolute right is the ability that underlies all the rest."

—Richard W. Wetherill
1906 - 1989

Contents

Preface

This book will teach you that there is a fail-safe life. You will discover how duty and desire become one, why pursuit of duty brings happiness and that real freedom comes from pursuing the Right-Action Ethic.

You will learn what Richard W. Wetherill discovered as teacher, lecturer, author and management consultant to leaders of business and industry for more than six decades. During that period, he wrote best-selling management material, including the first book on industrial foremanship, *Management Techniques for Foremen,* published by National Foremen's Institute, Inc. Other titles, published by D. Van Nostrand Co., include: *How to Succeed with People, How to Put Your Ideas Across* and *How to Get Leadership and Influence.*

Wetherill made the study of human behavior

his life's work, culminating in his trainees' giving birth to a highly successful business, based on those principles. Wetherill Associates, Inc. (WAI) of Royersford, Pennsylvania has grown from $1 million in sales in 1980 to about $80 million in 1992, by applying principles of right action. The result has brought deep personal satisfaction, job security and prosperity to hundreds of men and women whose lives he touched. They want to share the formula with everybody.

The fundamental premise of Wetherill's formula is that there is an objective moral Reality (capitalized to distinguish our use of the word from the more limited definition). This Reality, in Wetherill's thinking, resides in an all-powerful, natural law and is carefully differentiated from subjective, personal reality. Much like the force of gravity, the law of absolute right simply IS—invisible and impersonal, perhaps, but exerting mighty influence on our lives, whether we recognize it or not: Right action gets right results, whereas wrong action gets wrong results.

The good news is that Reality, as Wetherill defines it, is full of human possibility—possibility for change, for growth, for making reliable decisions, for creating a better world—so long, Wetherill says, as we recognize its absolute power in our lives.

Those people who have recognized the power of this objective, moral Reality (as opposed to their own self-centered, subjective reality) have been able to create lives and careers based on taking "right action." As a natural consequence, they are getting "right results."

As you read this book, you will embark on a voyage of self-discovery that may shock you, but it will also present a vision for you, for America and for the whole world community. In the process, you will be helping to ***put America on the right track!***

Introduction

Many popular writers warn that something in America has died. Perhaps so. But the leadership spirit of America will impact the whole wide world when business managers apply the leadership principles stated and illustrated on the pages of this book.

While it is true that America is at peace, the Cold War is over and the USSR is defunct, it is equally evident that, individually and collectively, choices are being compromised, prejudices preserved and financial hardships continue unrelieved.

The good news is that there is a shaft of light piercing the gloom—a light that will lead Americans into a new day of world leadership. This book is about that shaft of light. It is about performance, and when you read this book you will find it full of solutions based on principles as old as time itself but as new as the moment you live in. Readers will learn that what underlies family values and ethical behavior as well as financial success are basic principles guaranteed to work in every situation.

This book is not about a famous person or celebrity. You will not find famous quotes from well-known persons—past or present. It is a book about the experiences of ordinary people who are applying principles for successful living and, as a result, are enjoying huge success in their careers, with business associates, family members and one another. These principles were learned from Richard W. Wetherill, a man whose vision helped shape the lives of these ordinary people, and whose insights have shed a great light on the corporate pathway. It was his contact with reality that gave Wetherill the wisdom, counsel and ethical values that shaped his own life and the lives of his students.

Everybody can apply these principles to achieve an astonishing intellectual breakthrough. The principles of the Right-Action Ethic are the keystone of what is today a multimillion-dollar corporate success story: Wetherill Associates, Inc. (WAI) of Royersford, Pennsylvania.

This book shows you how taking right action creates personal joy, emotional health and professional success, and how ethical behavior by individuals raises the quality of life for businesses, families, communities, America and the world.

I am personally indebted to my friend and mentor Richard W. Wetherill for his inspiration, kindness, foresight and the principles he taught me. I want to pass along his insights into successful living to my own and the next generation, who will use these insights to provide leadership for a nation that is crying out for relief from its gripping problems.

At WAI, our management is strengthened by Mr. Wetherill's observation: "No person can long withstand the continued onslaught of carefully presented truth. It will finally compel recognition of error. It will finally reconcile the causes of misunderstanding and correct what is wrong."

E. Marie Bothe, President
WETHERILL ASSOCIATES, INC. (WAI)
Royersford, PA 19468

"Right decisions are found, not made."

—Richard W. Wetherill
Right Is Might

Chapter 1

Wetherill Associates, Inc. (WAI)

"It is a company policy to avoid all the nasty personality situations which tend to make people's working lives miserable. We find that it really can be done. We want everybody's cooperation in that effort. We trust that each and every person will do everything possible to make that policy keep on succeeding. Let this be a really happy place to work."

Richard W. Wetherill,
Former Chairman

Right-Action Ethic

From the moment you set foot inside the lobby of Wetherill Associates, Inc. (WAI) in Royersford, Pennsylvania, you are surrounded by a sense of calm and tranquility.

Missing is the air of frantic hustle and bustle, of tension and indifference. There is a curious air of innocence and unhurriedness as one is greeted by two young-at-heart ladies, seated at high-tech consoles with headsets—one in her late seventies, the other in her eighties—handling with complete calm a constant stream of calls. Their faces and body language show they are relaxed and happy in their work. Their smiles are real and their greetings to strangers are genuine and warm. You know they care about you and they care about the company they work for.

This is not the corporate America found on Market Street or Madison Avenue or the Chicago Loop. It is a kind of corporate America built on and directed by principles that most Americans know about, somewhere in their hearts and minds, yet fail to apply.

Wetherill Associates, Inc. (WAI), is a quintessential success story based on a dramatic growth pattern with a profitable bottom line in a time of financial recession. It demonstrates how the intent to do what each situation calls for—just because it is right—gets a successful result. It also allows employees from 18 to 90 to be a part of that success and enjoy its financial stability. WAI is a modern-day corporate success story, with a unique approach to leadership.

How it All Began

Wetherill Associates, Inc., began in 1978 when a woman from suburban Philadelphia, E. Marie Bothe, and others in Richard Wetherill's Behavioral Study Group, pooled their resources and set up shop as manufacturers' representatives for several major companies. In one bold move, WAI entered the rough-and-tumble world of the American automobile aftermarket industry where shady deals were often the norm.

But these people were prepared. For a number of years, the original 34 employees had listened to and absorbed the Right-Action Ethic of Richard W. Wetherill, their mentor and friend. In fact, for 20 years Bothe had been his right-hand assistant in bringing together members of his Behavioral Study Group. Now they were ready to put theory into practice in a business situation.

Wetherill, a longtime management consultant, first formed this Behavioral Study Group in 1950 to counter what he had seen as the disastrous consequences of wrong thinking, leading to wrong action and wrong results in the business world and in people's personal lives. Over the next quarter of a century, he worked with his associates and taught them to reason from reality rather than from their likes and dislikes when making decisions—a kind of scientific method applied to behavior. On July 21, 1978 Wetherill Associates, Inc., was incorporated at King of Prussia, Pennsylvania, 20 miles northwest of Philadelphia. The personnel was composed of senior citizens and middle-aged adults, but mostly of young people, barely out of their teens.

The fruits of Wetherill's labors were finally being realized. The seeds he had planted had germinated and had sprung into life as Wetherill Associates, Inc., a name that was chosen to honor Mr. Wetherill and provide incentive for all employees to perform at the highest level.

Reflecting on those early years, Bothe, president of WAI, admits that the company "fell" into the automotive aftermarket business because one member of the Study Group had had some experience in that field. In addition, research associates in other locations needed an employment opportunity so they could join Mr. Wetherill in the Philadelphia area.

The irony of their choice of business should not be lost. The automotive remanufacturing industry grew out of the junkyard business after World War II and was not known for its high ethical standards. Yet undaunted, the personnel had confidence in Wetherill's teachings and practiced the Right-Action Ethic against all odds. They enforced a no-gifts-accepted policy, refused to give kickbacks and, with the intent to do the right thing, dealt with customers honestly.

From their modest offices, the young sales staff began selling automotive parts by telephone. With virtually no telemarketing experience or training in modern sales techniques, they soon found themselves caught in a dilemma. Many of the companies WAI represented did not properly support their sales efforts. For example, WAI would provide customers quotes on parts, prices and delivery times, but the manufacturers they represented would not follow through as promised, and some companies were not supportive in other ways. More serious, several times WAI was forced to resort to the courts to be paid their commissions.

"To solve the problem, we began to stock our own parts and became distributors as well as representatives," Bothe recalls. As a result of that decision, the company began to grow and moved to larger quarters in King of Prussia—a converted warehouse that had once been a Lubin movie-set location where Toonerville Trolley and Marie Dressler comedies had been filmed in the 1920's.

Bothe describes this kind of business expansion as "management by reality." "As the reality called for expansion in warehouse space and number of employees to fill the needs of our customers, we expanded. It wasn't a goal we had set. Reality pushed us into it. That's why in 1986, we had to move to much larger quarters and developed a major warehousing operation in Royersford."

With its in-depth market research and technical training program, WAI connected customers and suppliers with attractive price structures by means of long-term, high-volume buying. Again when quality parts often could not be obtained in a timely fashion to supply its customers, WAI added a manufacturing capability to assemble starters and alternators on site.

The company went from $1 million in sales in 1980 to $17.6 million in 1985. Then, during a period when most businesses were downsizing, sales soared to nearly $70 million in 1991. By the third quarter of 1992, WAI realized a 22 percent increase over 1991! It is now one of the largest suppliers in its market.

Bothe recalls with nostalgia the company's first purchase order in 1980 of $5,000 for bearings. Present purchases of bearings are in excess of $12 million yearly. The company also became part of the international business community, importing and exporting products from and to the Far East, Australia, Britain, Europe, North Africa, South and Central America and Canada. In addition, WAI also established Regional Distribution Centers (RDC's) near Los Angeles, Atlanta, Chicago and Dallas to provide more timely delivery to its customers nationwide.

Sophisticated Engineering, Quality Control, Graphic Arts and Technical Training Departments were created and are now major departments in the corporation. Engineering and inspection detail documentation is currently being implemented for most of the 6,000 parts in the company's product line.

WAI is privately owned yet 100 percent of its profits are funneled back into the business to fund advanced research, inventory and equipment as well as to provide additional facilities, people, training, and employee benefits, to become debt free and to support local and national charities.

From a start-up group of 34, the company

grew to nearly 300 employees in 1992. As a part of his enlightened approach to corporate duties, Wetherill taught that while the science of accounting has no ledger pages for things such as jealousy, competition, company politics, empire building, snits, depression and frustration, these human conditions and activities are significantly responsible for corporate prosperity or failure.

In all departments, WAI's position is that if a contemplated wrong action such as lying would appear to give profitable results, then appearances are deceiving. (The long-term consequences would resemble what our national economy suffers from.) Conversely, if a right action would appear to produce a wrong result, again appearances are deceiving. (Long-term benefits would reflect the same economic strength as shown by WAI.) Company policy requires that employees take right action and not knowingly take wrong action. Every effort is made to debunk the fantasy that in the long-term net profit can result from wrong action or that net loss can result from right action.

Company Treasurer, Kevin Kraft, says, "We do not directly try to make profits or avoid losses.

Instead, we try to take right action as best we know how; the profits are a natural by-product."

Corporate Secretary and Director of Human Resources, Margo Callis, recognizes that her department is responsible for monitoring the quality of corporate life at WAI and that responsibility is considered fundamental.

"Cooperation is emphasized. Wrong behavior is given the same careful attention as defective product. Any low-quality behavior is treated as a mistake that is correctable with training and counseling," Callis observes. She also points out that prospective employees are screened for their ability to work well in an open, cooperative environment as well as for their professionalism or technical competence.

WAI has effectively met the challenge of expanding growth and profitability in recessionary times by using the Right-Action Ethic. With publication of this book and others written by Richard W. Wetherill, it is now poised to provide help and instruction on how to develop a similar result for the management and operation of any business or industry.

Management Philosophy

At the time the first phone calls were made by the young manufacturers' representatives at WAI in 1978, their thinking and training had been infused with the management methodology and teachings of Richard W. Wetherill. For over half a century Wetherill had written books, taught management courses and conducted training seminars for some of the nation's top companies, none of which accepted the whole package of right action and total honesty. At age 72, his influence and training in its entirety was focused directly on one company—WAI, where the Right-Action Ethic became its guiding light.

At a time when most of his contemporaries had retired from their business careers, Wetherill acted as the company's management consultant and training executive. For the first time, he was given the opportunity to demonstrate what constitutes truly successful leadership in the business world. His associates provided a corporation with a management team that put his behavioral principles into practice and began showing how the Right-Action Ethic inevitably works.

In a Quality Assurance Manual the company published in 1990, a year after Wetherill's death, his Right-Action Ethic is articulated in a three-fold formula for success:

- ***First, let every decision be made by consensus among the persons involved in accord with the dictates of reality and not by consensus of personal opinions.***
- ***Second, eliminate all considerations of personal ambition and private profit for a few.***
- ***Third, make sure that all thinking is centered on considerations of what is right for everybody—what will benefit the company as a whole, its customers, its suppliers, its employees and the community. Taken far enough these benefits would encircle the earth.***

All of the above reasoning is applied to everyday life at WAI and has won the respect and attention of WAI's customers in the automotive rebuilding industry here and abroad and of co-suppliers who are also competing for their business.

In subsequent chapters, the principles of the Right-Action Ethic Wetherill taught are given specific attention. They are the principles that have made WAI a leader in its field. There is nothing ivory tower or impractical about his program for success. It works for all who apply it in their careers as well as in their personal lives.

"Decisions are predetermined by relevant facts."

—Richard W. Wetherill
Right Is Might

Chapter 2

Doing the Right Thing

During the 1980's, America plunged into a decade of avarice and acquisitiveness. Interest rates soared, prices for commodities and housing skyrocketed. The financial future looked stable, but with the approach of the 1990's, fear set in. Banks and brokerage houses failed, corporations crumbled nearly overnight. A few individuals made billions of dollars, but in the process, the economy was weakened and upper management and middle management alike found themselves scrambling to seek other employment.

This economic downturn ushered in a period of downsizing. Bankruptcies soared, both personal and corporate, and millions were laid off as companies went under. The result was a recession described by some analysts as the worst since the Great Depression of 1929.

The truth is that the principles Richard

Wetherill taught and that are WAI's guiding light might have prevented what has come to pass if they had been implemented across the nation when they were presented decades ago. Unfortunately they were not.

Now America is facing economic decline, upheaval in its major cities, natural disasters and crises in health care. We must ask: Is there a set of principles, a management approach that can bring about economic and social healing and put America on the right track economically and morally? The answer is yes—it is the ***Right-Action Ethic.***

Richard Wetherill postulated that among all the lessons taught by history, the most important was that ***the forces of right ultimately triumph in every long-continued struggle.*** He taught that the forces of wrong are doomed to ultimate extinction as is evidenced in the lives of every tyrant and oppressor who ever trod this earth. But on a smaller scale, wrong action is also evident in the wrong results that people live with in their personal and professional lives—wrong results they blame on outside forces of one kind or another, because they cannot understand their own role in causing them.

The first step toward creating a successful and productive life is the willingness to do the right thing, to face life honestly and, in doing so, to face your own dishonesty. If you agree that it is wrong not only to lie, cheat and steal but also to neglect responsibilities, justify wrong behavior, try to manipulate others, insist on your way or do anything to hurt others, then you must look at yourself squarely and admit that you are doing some of those things.

If you are willing to become conscious of your own mistakes and make the decisions that follow, your life will dramatically change, and you will be led into an extraordinarily rewarding series of events: ***Be honest—take full responsibility for your own actions and face the truth about yourself—that is what matters.*** It is important for individuals to take this responsibility because every individual wrong has a detrimental effect on the common good. A world in which individual good in any way damages the common good does not make sense.

The first lesson Wetherill taught for successful living and a successful business then is this: If you, as one individual, are prepared to be honest in every decision you make, without compromise, you will lead the way into the benign revolution toward total honesty in our society. You will, as a natural consequence, benefit yourself and assume a leadership role in putting America on the right track.

To understand total honesty as an ingredient for doing the right thing, we should first discuss what stands in its way: dishonesty. Sadly, there are a number of people whose wrongs have done irrevocable damage from which there may be no escape. Many of us have, at the very least, made so many compromises that our view of total honesty has become distorted. In our society, dishonest habits such as justifying angry outbursts, criticizing and putting people down or projecting a false image have become so ingrained that the average person hardly knows what total honesty is. What is more revealing is that so many dishonest practices are now embodied in our public, private and business affairs. Happily most of us have the opportunity to change that destructive state of affairs by doing the right thing.

Wetherill stated that people fall into one of

four general categories. Perhaps you will see yourself in one of them.

- First, there are those who like and grow fat on the corrupt system of political graft and profits-at-any cost that already exists. If you know one such person, you will discover, before you read much further, that he is not so fortunate as he thinks.

- Second, there are those who feel caught in the system's vicious coils and consider it practical to go for the short-term advantage. But if the system changes, they will breathe a sigh of relief.

- Third, there are those who are indifferent and too callous to care what is going on. They invariably give support to the first group.

- Fourth, there are those who have broad moral scruples and try not to compromise them. They represent vital landmarks pointing to a better world.

Realistically we are in a situation where the

first group, the dishonest element, is firmly entrenched in our society. Moreover the indications are that violence, corruption and financial scheming and chicanery are on the rise.

If you feel, after reading this, that the situation seems utterly hopeless, don't despair. When you understand why people get into trouble, you will feel more sympathy than bitterness towards them, and therefore feel more inclined to help than to condemn them. The truth is: ***There are no bad people. There are people who make bad mistakes.***

There are also well-meaning people who are unintentionally dishonest in ways they do not suspect. For example, they may think it is right to fight for peace or do violence in support of a noble cause. They do not understand that it is always a mistake to fight and do violence, even for a cause that seems right. Wetherill found that there are more effective ways to right the wrongs of society.

Doing the right thing always has the best possible long-term outcome, but it may sometimes seem more difficult in the short term. For example, when WAI first entered the business community, it was regarded with derision and suspicion. Managers of other companies in the industry could not believe that honesty and right action were compatible with a healthy bottom line. The Right-Action Ethic was regarded by some as a gimmick or a ploy of subtle deviousness to gain market share. Those were the short-term obstacles, but the long-term rewards have been the good will, trust and respect WAI now enjoys in the domestic market as well as in countries as far away as Australia.

If you are called a goody-goody or hear rumors spread about the Right-Action Ethic, do not despair. WAI did nothing to defend itself against the wildest accusations, but instead continued to study customers' needs and to respond honestly with improved service, literature, quality—in other words to do the right thing. The long-term result is that WAI is a happy place to work, has enthusiastic customers, cooperative suppliers, friendly competitors, and a broad reputation for integrity and "having it all together." In addition, its executives and managers are free of the typical burdens that seem insurmountable in most corporations.

While it may be true that you cannot change human nature, we do know it is possible to change people's thinking, and through that, their conversation and behavior so that, by doing the right thing, total honesty can be achieved. To do that, in his book *Right Is Might,* Wetherill specifically describes two ways to change people's thinking. One is by persuasion, and the other is by force. Personal force is ruled out as part of the Right-Action Ethic. Wetherill points out that the old adage is still true: A man convinced against his will is of the same opinion still. But persuasion works, and the simplest and most effective kind of persuasion is that of good example. WAI's business record provides an example to encourage others to try the Right-Action Ethic.

Since persuasion is needed to inspire voluntary action, persuasion must offer some personal advantage or gain, or conversely it must enable a person to avoid some personal trouble or loss.

An example Wetherill often used: If you are standing on a railroad track and someone shouts, "A train is coming!" you would act on his word and get off the track. But if no one apprised you of your danger, the sight of the track and approaching train would cause you to jump. In other words, the reality would provide the motivation.

The victims of dishonest, wrong thinking are in much the same position. They do not see its danger, and the attempted warning in this book may be ignored. But if you look at the reality of what is happening on all sides, the evidence is clear that too many wrong results are bearing down on us. The good news is that applying the Right-Action Ethic will virtually stop your vulnerability to wrong results, take the effort out of your exertions and enable you to do what you want to do, to the exclusion of what you don't want to do. Because you want to do the right thing, you are put on the right track.

One persuasive method of inducing a change to right action is by depriving someone of a desired opportunity unless that change is made. Sometimes that kind of change will come only through sheer economic necessity. At WAI, a condition of employment is that employees agree to take right action and refrain from taking wrong action. If an applicant needs the job, as most persons do these days, he or she will agree to the Right-Action Ethic. When mistakes occur (and they will), the employee is reminded of the right-action policy and counseled as to how that mistake can be corrected.

The following example illustrates the use of that form of persuasion: Our sales and purchasing people sometimes have to deal with irate callers. Right action requires them not to resist but to let the person on the other end vent his emotion and state his case. There may be various reasons for the caller's outburst that do not even relate to the transaction. Maybe a valued worker just quit, or he learned that his wife smashed his car.

Wetherill taught that such emotion can be reciprocal. If you listen for the information and remain calm, the caller's emotion dies because you are not resisting or supporting it. A rational discussion can then disclose the reality, and complaints are effectively resolved. Try it next time someone tries to engage you in an argument. Just as you can smother a fire by cutting off its oxygen, a fire between or among people is smothered by withdrawing your emotional input.

Over the years in his lectures, Wetherill made it clear that emotional reactions work against a person's best interests. "Emotion," he said, "destroys rationality and sends thinking off in a wrong direction." But how does a person drop his emotion when it bubbles up?

Wetherill provided his students with a technique which they, in turn, have passed along to others. While appearing childlike to some, it is effective.

Here is the technique: When emotion wells up and swirls in your mind, picture a battleship riding on a calm sea. Throw in some moonlight so that a dive bomber becomes visible in your mental picture. Watch while the plane drops bombs on the ship so that it explodes into thousands of pieces of debris floating on the surface of the water. Add some sound effects (so long as it doesn't disturb anyone near you) and enjoy the release of emotional tension.

Some people picture a steam valve fastened at their wrists. They turn the petcock, and the steam escapes in a hissing cloud—so does their emotion. Others visualize popcorn kernels in their cupped hands that suddenly pop until their hands are empty. Almost any mental picture of that kind can be used to drain off emotion.

As one salesperson reported, "You know, it works."

In the effort to do the right thing, you can withdraw patronage from a store or withhold your vote or refuse to carry out the dishonest instructions of a superior. Your actions might count as only one factor, but it is surprising how often that factor is decisive.

A lot of dishonesty in business continues only because it is supported and protected by people in surrounding positions. Yet even though mass dishonesty continues, WAI demonstrates that it takes just a few people using the Right-Action Ethic to alter the balance of power. You will find it is usually easy to gain recruits for any clearly stated, sound moral cause.

Another way to handle dishonesty in direct dealings with another person is to state the truth. When that occurs, one of two things ordinarily happens. Either the dishonest person changes his thinking, or he is replaced. At WAI, we have learned that an honest person can succeed easily in relation to a dishonest person on the wrong track. It may require time, but honest people have the force of right working for them.

Furthermore, when you get into the habit of doing the right thing, you will discover that ***direct competition, even in a capitalist economy, is no longer a necessary part of success. Every right purpose can be served without it.***

As you read further, you will understand that ***no aggressive action is needed*** to secure a victory for the forces of right. In the meantime, those persons who have already provided the patterns of good influence and example find that their lives flourish as a result. As Wetherill states in *Right Is Might,* they, and perhaps you, will have demonstrated that ***right will eventually prevail as the eternal basis of might.***

"The person who lives the Right-Action Ethic benefits everybody on earth. He will benefit posterity. Before he benefits anyone else, he benefits himself, because he has a dynamic formula for successful accomplishment."

—Richard W. Wetherill
Right Is Might

Chapter 3

An Infallible Formula for Success

There is a crisis in business ethics today that is unparalleled in the publicity given it by the American news media. Managers are cutting ethical corners for short-term profits; employees are stealing from their employers both in product, lost days and costly overtime, and, worst of all, they are all rationalizing it. Top managers are firing employees to pump up profits for the short term while compensation for top executives keeps spiraling upward.

The tendency for doing the wrong thing has proven costly. Dozens of corporations are facing mandatory fines that reach into the hundreds of millions for a broad range of crimes that include antitrust violations, breaking securities and contract laws, fraud, discrimination, unsafe practices, bribery, and money laundering. The end results are not only more and more law firms but a loss of something vital to the nation: moral conscience, faith, and trust.

Deeply troubled by the unethical behavior that he saw even fifty years ago, Wetherill, then in his mid-forties, formed a Behavioral Study Group to counter the disastrous consequences of that wrong thinking. He taught the group that under the right circumstances if a person follows and practices the Right-Action Ethic consistently, he can change his life: ***Always think, say and do what is right; refuse to think, say or do what is wrong.***

But there are requirements to be met. A person cannot decide he or she is sole arbiter of what is right without regard for the consequences of his or her behavior in the lives of others. While this is not intended to relate to legal entanglements, it does relate to behavioral entanglements that are essentially moral.

To avoid such entanglements puts no restrictions on anybody's freedom. Instead their avoidance makes genuine freedom possible. What is more important, to apply the Right-Action Ethic you need common sense, not blind or unquestioning faith. You may not live it perfectly, but it is the ideal, and if you consistently apply it to yourself, rather than being restricted, you will gain genuine freedom.

Like an electric light switch that sends power to light up a room, the mental switch that produces ethical enlightenment is found in the formula: ***Always think, say and do what is right; refuse to think, say or do what is wrong.***

If you apply this formula, your life will be transformed, and you will be making a contribution to the freedom and safety of all other fellow beings. In a world filled with conflict and distress, if you live by this formula, you will function with complete calm. Nothing will disturb your inner emotional balance. You won't have to seek peace of mind because you will have it! But you will not have on mental blinders about the state of the world nor be able to ignore the troubles of society and pretend that all's well. You will be a realist. You will know what is going wrong and will be doing something constructive about it.

You will be living the Right-Action Ethic. You will choose to meet life head on because your skills, energies and ingenuity will be constantly challenged by the opportunities and events of life.

Furthermore, adoption of the Right-Action Ethic will relieve you of vocational troubles. Whatever you attempt will work out. Life will open up before you and present you with every opportunity you need. You will not be called on to serve contradictory purposes or interests, be in two places at once, suffer from anxiety or depression—not while you live in accord with the principle of absolute right found in the Right-Action Ethic: ***Always think, say and do what is right; refuse to think, say or do what is wrong.***

Do you want to be such a person? You can. It's a matter of choice. Do not be diverted by anyone who says, "Sometimes it doesn't pay to do the right thing." The simple fact is that doing the right thing always pays. The only way to get into trouble is to do the wrong thing.

"It's not expedient," someone else might say. That is untrue. The terms right and expedient are identical in meaning.

Always do the right thing. Right action leads to right results. Wrong action leads to wrong results. Right action cannot lead to wrong results. Wrong action cannot lead to right results. Right can never contradict proper duty; all are identical by definition.

At this point, you may be skeptical, but the day has arrived when there are many people who realize that the principle of absolute right is the crux of man's relationship to man, and also man's relationship to God. The members of Wetherill's Study Group have experienced a renewal of purpose for their lives and are serving that higher purpose to do what is right as best they can.

As you read this, you know in what areas you have to make sound moral choices. Once you have done that, extend those areas out. That will give you more freedom because then you will have fewer kinds of troubles. You will recognize that ***morality consists of recognizing and doing what is right while recognizing and refusing to do what is wrong.***

A true statement is one that is in exact accord with the facts. A little wrong is as wrong as a big wrong. It is as wrong, for example, to steal one cent as it is to steal a million dollars. One wrong may lead to more serious consequences than another, nevertheless, any wrong is wrong.

Whatever your goals and desires in life are, don't let them dominate your thinking. Remember: ***Think, say and do what is right; refuse to think, say or do what is wrong.***

When you adopt the Right-Action Ethic, even as an experiment, your troubles will start correcting themselves. A new light will shine in your eyes, a new spring will rise in your step and a new buoyancy will result from shedding conscious and unconscious burdens. Even in a crisis when there is no time to plan, you will tend to take right action. In the crunch you will instinctively resort to doing what is right. And that is what matters.

Make the resolve: "Hereafter, I shall ***intentionally*** do what is right!"

Chapter 4

Improving Working Relationships

While lecturing, Wetherill spelled out his ideas about how to improve working relationships, a necessary component of effective leadership. What follows is an edited version of one of his lectures.

In every business or industrial situation, executives are constantly being forced to use one of two kinds of authority. One is technical authority, the other is disciplinary authority. Technical authority is the authority a supervisor or manager uses in instructing subordinates how to do their work and meet their job obligations. It is essentially nonbehavioral authority exercised over technical activity.

Disciplinary authority, on the other hand, is the kind of authority a supervisor or executive uses in making what he or she thinks are critical corrections in the behavior of employees. As he is the boss, so is he the disciplinarian. He not only tells employees how to do their work, he must also tell them, at times, to stop and correct their wrong behavior.

When technical problems arise, unintentional mistakes are the cause and are easily corrected. When behavioral problems arise, however, there is usually an intentional effort on someone's part to get the upper hand or get out of a position that has lost its advantage.

It's important to note that a technical problem is not solved on a behavioral basis. It is solved by identifying and correcting the method or process. In the field of engineering, for example, the laws of physics strictly control how the engineering is to be done.

It is in the behavioral field that the baffling problems develop. Even when the problems relate to technical matters, if there is conflict, that conflict is always behavioral in nature. A lot of conflict finds its way into conversation about technical matters. When that occurs, there is a split system, partly technical and partly behavioral. Wetherill taught that there is no such thing as a purely technical conflict. As a very young man, Wetherill discovered that the law of absolute right, ***Right action gets right results, whereas wrong action gets wrong results,*** applies to behavioral problems as inevitably as the laws of physics apply to engineering problems.

For example, if an employee competes with you for the purpose of getting the upper hand, he may try to do the job his way to show how smart he is. At that point technical guidance is rejected and behavioral conflict is inserted.

What has happened is that a behavioral problem has complicated a technical problem because competition for control has now taken over. What is needed is to separate the technical problem from the behavioral problem. At WAI when a technical mistake is made, a careful analysis usually reveals that the reason for it is behavioral rather than technical. Knowing this can direct your attention to the real underlying problem.

Most managers, supervisors and executives in either business or vocational employment know that behavioral problems cause the greatest amount of trouble, wrecking people's careers, sometimes even their lives. When this happens, it becomes the biggest human-resource tragedy in a company.

All such behavioral problems are correctly defined as conflict. They directly contribute to other problems that arise such as excessive financial burdens, low morale, empire building, high employee turnover, stress, chronic fatigue, even stomach ulcers and more.

Technical Counseling

Technical problems can be illustrated by the making of a blueprint or in making the product that the blueprint describes. Even putting a stamp on an envelope is a technical problem, so it is easy to see that the authority for technical problems is reality itself. All technical work is based on reality, or it does not succeed.

Technical problems that arise out of reality will always be a part of normal business or industrial operations. When a high-tech corporation comes out with a better computer than its competitor, the competition's staff sets about looking into the technical achievements involved. Technical problems are often temporary, because each new achievement is a stepping-stone to further achievements.

Wrong impressions of a technical nature are relatively easy to identify and fix. Suppose, for example, that a worker is rushing to do a job, and you criticize him for his haste. When he explains that he has to be finished by 3 o'clock that day, you can correct his wrong impression by saying you meant 3 o'clock the next day. Does the worker go on hurrying the same way? Of course not. That is an example of a minor technical problem. No behavioral problem is at stake. Technical problems are easy to straighten out and require little attention to fix. Once the reality is seen, you can immediately take the confusion out of the situation.

It is clear that everybody uses the authority of reality in nonbehavioral problems. For instance, if a key is used to unlock a door, a simple trial determines whether it works or doesn't. This is using the authority of reality in a nonbehavioral way. When a person discovers the reality that he is using the wrong key, he gives up trying to unlock the door with it. Reality is the final arbiter.

Behavioral Counseling

Wrong impressions are easily correctable when they relate to technical problems, unless people let behavioral considerations interfere. If you are a line executive or supervisor, you should be free to concentrate on technical work, but at times you will be forced to devote attention to disciplinary problems. No matter how capable you are in the technical side of your work, you will have difficulty solving behavioral problems. It may take an outside counselor to do that.

It should also be noted that when executives and supervisory staff are sidetracked into dealing with the emotional reactions that trigger behavioral problems, they become the victims of distress. This distress causes an emotional disturbance that often has the effect of endangering the entire company's safety by diverting attention from the requirements of reality that keep the business healthy. Anyone reading these pages knows that behavioral problems cause the great bulk of vocational problems. These same behavioral problems sink many an industrial ship and wreck many a promising career.

For this reason, executives will find it best to turn behavioral problems over to people who are skilled in handling them. These people have clear thinking and can bypass virtually all personality considerations. When the counselor has the proper skills and understands the situation, he or she can easily dispose of problems without being irritated by them in the way a manager may be irritated.

Having applied Mr. Wetherill's procedures at WAI, we know that if you follow them, you can revolutionize not only your working relationships, but all your other relationships as well.

In business and industry most behavioral problems get settled by the intervention of a person in a position of higher authority—especially if he has the power to fire someone who will not give in. That higher authority does not even have to be right. That is the nature of human authority, and it is always artificial.

No behavioral problem should ever be solved on the sole basis of human authority. In dealing with behavioral problems as with technical problems, we should always resort to the higher authority of reality. The information found in the reality should always be the deciding factor in dealing with all behavioral problems. In fact, this principle is so important that to be an effective counselor you do not need to have "official" authority at all. When an authority figure tries to be the person who deals with a behavioral problem as the counselor, his authority may actually be a handicap.

When decision making is done on the basis of reality, the authority of individuals becomes irrelevant. To be fully effective, that is the way counseling should always be done. When personal authority is exerted, it spoils the prospect of allowing the authority of reality to become visible.

Since most people are inclined to use personal authority in relation to behavioral problems, that complicates things almost every time. It becomes a battle of wills: "I want it done my way." "No, I'm going to do it my way." Resorting to personal authority explains most of the conflicts in the workplace, at home and in national and international affairs. Furthermore we are going to keep on having such conflicts until the story of behavioral reality is understood everywhere.

In the behavioral field, few people want to look at the appropriate reality, and that is the reason we have behavioral problems. Because these problems are customarily dealt with on the basis of conflict and competition, it is not surprising they do not yield to treatment.

Human authority is used in dealing with behavioral problems in phrases such as: "If you do that again, I'll fire you," "Stop that or I'll smack you down" or "You'll give in to me, or you'll wish you had." Human authority? Perhaps we should say inhuman authority.

In any counseling situation that you want to resolve, reality must be seen. When it is not clear, business and industrial counselees should ask, "What is it that I do that makes you describe me that way?" Of course, ideally you should have carefully described the counselee's behavior without being asked. When he or she has to ask, it demonstrates a failure to provide certain of the information that would have directed everybody's attention to the reality.

No matter how careful the participants are, such problems can and do arise; it is easy to make a mistake. If so, a mistake is easily corrected. However, when the resistance is intentional, anything can happen.

If either the counselee or counselor fails to understand the contributing factors that caused the counseling to be needed, each should make inquiries of the other.

Nobody ever attempts to defend himself or herself in relation to a technical problem unless it spills over into a behavioral problem. The technical action is either right or wrong. Attack and defense have nothing whatever to do with the outcome unless a behavioral problem intervenes. When it does, since people compete and are jealous of one another, behavioral problems almost always intrude because one of the parties wants his own way. When that happens, a technical problem is turned into a behavioral problem, and the end result is trouble.

Whether a problem is technical or behavioral, people, rightly or wrongly, are forced to reason from the impressions they have formed. They cannot do anything else. The counseling should disclose the overlooked reality so that impressions are corrected. Wrong impressions of a technical nature are readily correctable so long as behavioral problems do not interfere to complicate matters. When they do, only the facts of the situation will resolve the misunderstanding.

At WAI a situation developed during a period when the warehouse departments were being moved to other locations within the warehouse. It was a hot, muggy day in early summer. Two department heads found themselves at odds over where the line should be drawn to physically separate their departments. Each thought he needed the larger space. Antagonism mounted and angry words were exchanged until a counselor with Wetherill training stepped into the fray. Without pulling rank, the counselor immediately defused the emotion by stating points of reality in the situation: the need for larger space by one department, the fact that the move was a temporary step and that a safety factor was involved. The technical solution became immediately obvious when statements of reality removed the emotion from the discussion.

Under ordinary circumstances, two good working friends could have been driven permanently apart by emotional grudges aimed at each other. Instead, each one sheepishly faced his own wrong behavior, and both came out winners. So did the company. Commonly most solutions to these problems are imposed on the basis of human authority with such words as, "Just do as I say," or "This is the way it is going to be," or "There will be no further discussion; my decision is final." The truth is, that approach neither solves nor resolves anything; it simply perpetuates problems by suppressing them.

When behavioral problems arise between a person in a supervisory position and a subordinate, they can produce antagonistic feelings that put a blight on communication between those two persons. When a supervisor is confronted by an antagonistic employee, it is better to have a third party step in to handle the problems to avoid damage to the welfare of the business. The outside mediator can take the heat out of the disagreement between them.

The way behavioral problems are truly solved, of course, is not by technical means. It is by applying the Right-Action Ethic and dropping the wrong behavior causing the problem.

It is important to release persons in key positions in the company from the necessity to deal with behavioral problems. Of course, in some cases the problems can be disposed of quickly in a sentence or two. In these cases, because of the nature of the misunderstanding, almost anybody available can work out those problems efficiently and with little rancor. However, the energies of key persons in the company should be used for the technical problems that relate primarily to the reality of the way the business should run.

Precautions

When behavioral counseling goes astray, one or the other or both of two reasons are responsible: Either important information was left out or incorrect information was included. This happens by accidental misunderstanding or by intent.

However, there is a much more serious problem that is nearly always present. It is so common that it is rarely seen as a problem, although it is the real reason why people have so much trouble giving and receiving counseling. It relates to something that deserves to be called "brutality" but is not thought of in that sense. We hear a lot today about police brutality, spousal brutality, brutality of children and sexual brutality. However, there is a thread of brutality that is woven through virtually all human relationships that is rarely thought of as such. Increasingly such brutality is the rule rather than the exception in our dealings with one another.

An example of such brutality was witnessed recently in a local sales organization—not WAI. At a meeting of the sales staff, the top salesperson was applauded, praised and awarded a prize for his high sales. When the cheering had stopped, the bottom salesperson was announced so that everybody attending the meeting could pelt that person with Styrofoam wafers provided for the purpose. Don't shake your head in disbelief—it really happened. Such methods might generate more sales in the short term, but in the long term, they impose emotional damage and scars and increase employee turnover.

In a limited sense, such brutality gets carried over into every counseling session until people learn to avoid it. It tends to persist even when efforts are made to keep it out, and it constitutes the deepest reason why most counseling fails to achieve genuine success. While the brutality referred to is usually only verbal abuse, nevertheless, harsh words and tones of voice are inescapably damaging to working relationships.

In order for counseling to be effective, it is essential to get rid of the attack tactics so prevalent in interpersonal relationships: belittling, putdowns, squelches, sarcastic or snide remarks. The correct procedure is simply to fill in all the details of reality, which will have the effect of eliminating the emotional details that have developed. It is easy enough to do. If you try to do it, you ***will*** do it. If you do not do it, it is because you are trying to do something else.

Participants have to limit themselves to the requirements of reality with no personal reactions. You have to listen to correct information; you have to listen to incorrect information. You must be prepared to reason the information to the ground, determine what the reality is and then base your decisions on that reality.

People are sometimes afraid to try this approach, but fear has only one intelligent use: to turn attention in the right direction. Everybody should be afraid to deviate from reality in any detail of his thinking or conversation or behavior. Of course, both you and the counselee can make mistakes. However, a promptly corrected mistake is not serious.

On the whole, emotional reactions can be used as a signal that the steps required for successful counseling are not being followed. The moment someone begins to attack or defend his position, you will know that the counseling program has gone off the track, and it will not succeed until it gets back on the right track.

Nobody will ever attack another or defend himself when he sees all the reality correctly; instead he is guided by that reality.

There is no need for emotion in dealing with technical problems. Behavioral problems, on the other hand, generate emotion and are virtually impossible to deal with successfully in the presence of that emotion. It can be truly said that if there is no emotion, there is no behavioral problem. You need to know that it is emotion that clouds a person's intelligence, makes him eager to do something he should not do and confuses him so that he does not see anything wrong with it.

It must be understood that the same emotion that pushes a person toward wrong action blinds him intellectually so that he cannot see the wrongness. Typically, he does not want to see it. He wants to win his point.

Since emotional reactions have to be eliminated completely to resolve behavioral problems, your thinking has to be based entirely on reality and not on urges based on personal desires. It can be done by applying the Right-Action Ethic and letting reality lead the way.

"Each individual doing what he knows is right and refusing to do what he knows is wrong ensures a secure future."

—Richard W. Wetherill
Right Is Might

Chapter 5

Leadership Into the 21st Century

This book is about leadership in business and indeed life itself. It is about how to develop leadership qualities, starting from a whole new set of premises that people have customarily failed to consider. You will discover that to think, say and do the right thing is as essential to leadership in the business of running a successful company as it is in family and community life.

In recent years dozens of books on the subject of leadership have appeared on the shelves of the nation's bookstores. Several have reached best-seller status. With few exceptions common threads can be found woven throughout them all. They are these: There is a vacuum in leadership in America. Celebrities are not leaders. Leaders are made, not born. Leaders have vision, wisdom and often a personal power that is attractive and appealing to their followers.

In this book, you will find a new approach to leadership—dynamic and "doable"! Richard Wetherill understood that true leadership is expressed when you make it your intent to ***let yourself be led by reality.*** Leadership is achieved by following the path that reality plots as you think, say and do the right thing and refuse to do the wrong thing.

In this final chapter you will learn why real leaders are in such short supply. Wetherill's message here deals directly with what constitutes leadership and the skills necessary to manage people.

Since the Industrial Revolution, the usual model in business leadership has been hierarchical: top-down leadership. Business tycoons who amassed great fortunes, for instance, were autocratic, domineering, and used personal pressure to get the job done. The end result, however, was often disgruntled employees, inferior products and the necessity for labor unions. While not every business and industrial leader was like that, this model prevailed in most businesses.

In his book, *How to Get Leadership and Influence,* Wetherill shows that the basic ingredient of true leadership is a guiding standard, a standard that will carry an ordinary person to the highest level of leadership and reward him with feelings of deep satisfaction for a job well-done.

You can find that standard in the infallible formula: ***Think, say and do what is right.*** If that formula is followed, all the other requirements will fall into place. Also present will be a sense of integrity and a kind of sixth sense to know what each situation calls for. That guiding standard of doing what is right can be found at WAI. And it works.

Wetherill defines integrity as honesty with self, candor with others and maturity of attitude. Integrity is the basis of trust, which is not so much an ingredient of leadership as it is a natural product. Integrity is a quality that develops in the leader when he follows the "right" path.

Wetherill understood that in dealing with reality, a person is dealing with the ***only*** viable force able to change people's behavior from wrong to right action. In making that change from wrong to right, character is formed, people's lives improve and corporations are turned around. This kind of character is as vital in a leader as energy and competence. Energy and competence do not replace vision and character. It is not enough for a leader to do things right; he must ***do the right thing.***

Wetherill taught that to all his students. Nearly all the young men and women who formed WAI initially (most of whom are still with the company) had formerly endured deeply troubled lives, many with ingrained and addictive behaviors that needed to be dealt with and expunged before they could be given leadership roles. Over the few months Wetherill counseled them, their lives straightened out. They stopped smoking, drinking, doing drugs, vandalizing, defying authority and engaging in risky sex. Now they are leaders. By reasoning from reality, they conquered their fears, self-doubts, and addictive behaviors. Today they stand as models of rectitude, humbled by past experiences, grateful for the healing in their lives, and leading a corporation that will possibly rank in the top 1000 U.S. corporations in the 21st century.

Most executives today will argue that the average worker does not possess leadership ability. Wetherill had a different view. He said that while the average worker showed little evidence of abilities to lead, he does innately possess them, and if stimulated, his leadership abilities will develop. While acknowledging that many workers do not desire positions of leadership, lack ambition and would rather avoid the problems of responsibility, Wetherill makes the point that people are forced, at one time or another during their lives, to play leadership roles. The leadership may only be needed to fulfill family obligations or simply participate at social gatherings, but it is there.

According to government statistics, a high percentage of American businesses employ fewer than ten workers so the majority of business owners have only a small handful of employees to direct. But if a person asks any sort of question, he is looking to someone else for leadership. In fact, whenever you give another person guidance or offer direction (even to a family member), provide training, correct people's mistakes, induce people to try harder, stimulate them to think more, give instructions or orders, improve confidence or morale, you are exercising leadership.

Wetherill wrote that truly effective leadership could better be characterized as ***guidance.*** "Using the word guidance," he said, "deflects the instinct for power inherent in most relationships. People who try to exert leadership most often get into trouble. Egos clash, motives contradict and opposition from competitors is stimulated. People who directly assume the title of 'leader' invite repercussions, and hurdles appear that could otherwise have been avoided. Furthermore, the person who blatantly asserts his leadership will be tempted to focus attention on himself rather than on the action that should be taken. ***To be a successful leader, a person should think primarily of guiding others to do the right thing.***

"By using the concept of guidance, you are also less likely to impose your will on someone else, and because it also carries no flavor of intimidation, you invite little resistance. Above all, it carries with it the preservation of the other person's dignity."

As an example, Wetherill cited an instance in which, while driving up a mountain road, he encountered a motorist trying to jack up his ditched car. As the man worked, the jack kept driving deeper into the mud. "When I saw his dilemma I immediately offered to help. Methodically I started collecting stones to build a foundation for the jack. Suddenly my wife leaned out the window of our car and shouted, 'Why don't you get all these men to just lift the car back on the roadway?'

'What men?' I snorted.

"To my surprise I looked up and saw a semicircle of men watching my labors. They had left their cars and walked ahead to see what was blocking them. About a dozen immediately stepped forward, and we lifted the car back onto the roadway.

"Here is what this story demonstrated. Let reality govern the situation. Unless your guidance affords the best available means of meeting a situation, it will be easy for somebody else to supplant your leadership. Moreover, it will be to your advantage to let him do it.

"By popular consent my wife had been placed in the leadership position. Because she was alert to what was going on, she produced the ideal solution to the problem, and nobody resented her intrusion. Everybody benefited by the result."

From this encounter, we learn several things. The first is that the relative position or status, intelligence or authority of any of the participants may be irrelevant to the situation. Secondly the person who gives correct guidance is in contact with reality and is the one who knows what ought to be done. Everybody else falls into line.

While admittedly it may be harder to get your guidance accepted by someone who considers himself your superior; nevertheless when that guidance is urgently needed, carefully conceived and well presented, it will get results.

A case in point is a child who is sent to bed for obstreperous behavior in the presence of guests. Thirty minutes later the child appears and says through his tears, "Even if you spank me again, I have to tell you the bathroom curtain is on fire!" This is an example of a child, in a subordinate position, exerting his will against his parents' expressed wish. Everybody present is thankful for the child's courage.

In this same way, managers should let subordinate employees lead when they have the necessary information. Wetherill makes the point that a person who has a superior position in a business situation does not really need to exert his authority at all; he can get best results entirely by eliciting voluntary cooperation. Authority is usually understood as the right to demand obedience, and to be fully effective, it must be backed up by the threat to use force. Since authority in business or industry cannot be backed up by physical force or violence, the worst you can do is to fire the person. But by firing an employee, you admit an inability to direct him or her.

The truth is, punishment and the threat of punishment are tools of fear. They are substitutes for effective leadership. In a sense, they are instruments of slavery and dictatorship. If an employee sufficiently objects, he could find another job or file a grievance.

In an ideal organization no discipline is ever used. And a leader who stimulates voluntary cooperation from his employees will inevitably get better results than one who persists in using an approach that expresses brutality.

As a leader you should avoid saying and doing what your workers will resent. Instead find ways to stimulate their interest, imagination and enthusiasm. That approach will release their higher energies and creative abilities. You will discover that the worker who wants to do a good job will almost invariably prove more productive than the one who has to.

Wetherill states that, in his experience, when enlightened management policies guided employees through leadership rather than "drivership," the result was an increase in production levels by as much as 30 percent.

We can only conclude that what the average leader or supervisor urgently needs is not more discipline but more *disciples.* The question is, how to get them?

Wetherill defined authority as the ability to command confidence and respect because you deserve them through your own competence and reliability. You can use that kind of authority to get voluntary cooperation by stimulating employees' ambitions and pointing their abilities in the direction of constructive results. To obtain the best from your employees, your authority must rest on a sense of competence and personal effectiveness rather than on raw power backed by disciplinary force.

When you use the authority of competence, you can sit on the sidelines and run a business without seeming to be the boss. Wetherill recounts the story of a man who bought a business and conducted it in this manner for almost a year before his employees found out he was the new owner. "I wanted to get a line on what was happening, and I also wanted to earn the employees' confidence in advance, to be sure the news that I was the new chief would come as no shock." As a leader, when your subordinates' first desire is to please you ***by doing the right thing***, you will have no trouble with discipline.

Conventional wisdom has it that authority is the right to demand obedience based on your ability to threaten and deliver actual punishment. Authority in this sense is delegated by stockholders to a board of directors to the officers and executives to the lowest supervisor. Delegated authority of the conventional kind, to be effective, must carry real not implied power. If you don't have delegated authority, don't try to use it; somebody might call your bluff. It is good self-discipline to exercise your own ability to stimulate voluntary cooperation, and when you can do this at will, it won't matter whether you have delegated authority or not. Anybody can swing a club, but it takes real leadership ability to get along without one. It gets great results, too!

The key to real leadership is to emphasize your responsibilities rather than your authority, and develop your faculty for carrying out those responsibilities well. Get people to do as they should by making them *want* to, and you will have a really universal tool for getting things done.

In his book, *How To Get Leadership and Influence,* Wetherill stated that there were universal problems in human relationships and universal solutions to those problems.

He pointed out that if you conduct each relationship with due regard for the principles of the Right-Action Ethic, you will have little trouble. You will, he said, create unending opportunities to succeed, not only for yourself but also for the people with whom you deal. When you practice the Right-Action Ethic, you can expect the best of your employees, and with proper encouragement, determine what may be blocking them to release them from that blockage, enabling them to perform to their full capacity.

WAI's attitude is that if you channel people into the right departments you can expect great things from them. They will, in return, give you the best they can.

At WAI, Callis says, "That doesn't mean we are foolish about what we can expect from people. We stretch people; we don't strain them. At every turn in the road, we look at the reality of the situation and let that determine our decisions. We try to let reality govern everything."

When someone looks at WAI, one is astounded by the fact that few of its leaders and managers have had much formal business training. Here is a corporation with sales of $80 million, growing by leaps and bounds, run by people who have complete confidence in the Right-Action Ethic. They are not harried and work with smiles on their faces. While many of them barely made it through high school, their ability to follow the path reality has laid out for them provides the guidance they need.

Some of their backgrounds would give serious

pause to employment officers in major corporations. But WAI is different. The Right-Action Ethic Richard Wetherill taught not only gives these people a new outlook on life, it has lifted them up to levels of thinking and leadership that would make directors of business schools around the country draw their breath. They are making it work, and they enthusiastically regard their day-to-day activities as the unfolding of a master plan that will bring peace on earth as everybody learns to adhere to the Right-Action Ethic.

Ms. Callis, whose life was in chaos before she met Wetherill, openly admits that he put her on her feet. And the result? She now heads the Department of Human Resources at WAI and is responsible for the smooth coordination of nearly 300 people. She has taught herself how to use computers, talks confidently about settling disputes between employees by directing attention to Right Action, gives confidence to the apprehensive, reassures the self-doubters, focuses employees' strengths in areas where they are best suited and has implemented the Right-Action Ethic in her marriage as well as on the job.

You, too, can become one of these Wetherill-trained leaders poised for the future. You can be strong, confident and ready, when you adopt the style of reality leadership that guarantees to maximize not only your own strengths but the strengths of those you work and live with.

In today's corporate culture, every policy change molds the company's style of doing business. While this is often thought of as abstract and unimportant, that style has significant impact on everything that occurs in the company. The corporate culture, therefore, can determine the company's long-term survival—or demise.

At WAI the underlying culture is devoted to doing what is right and refusing to think, say or do what is wrong. When the Right-Action Ethic is understood and practiced, everything else falls into place. The bottom line takes care of itself as a natural by-product. Because harmony prevails, productivity is automatically high. No one is pushing anybody—reality is the boss.

The following outline on "Leadership" from Wetherill's *Management Techniques for Foremen* provides guidelines for gaining a leadership role.

Apply each sentence to your own situation, and you will find sidelights and implications turning on in your mind.

1. Develop your workers' confidence in your leadership:
   A. Constantly give your workers training that will improve their ability
   B. Treat each person as an individual
   C. Let each individual know how he stands with you
   D. Never block anyone's progress
   E. Treat each worker with respect
   F. Make judicious use of criticism and praise.
2. Keep your workers feeling good about their jobs:
   A. Show plenty of enthusiasm yourself
   B. Set performance levels to stretch each worker's ability
   C. Let each worker know that you value his ideas

D. Protect your workers from unpleasant surprises

E. Never make an unreasonable request

F. Hold the Right-Action Ethic as incentive for workers.

3. Go out of your way to stimulate favorable attitudes:

A. Think and talk in constructive, favorable terms

B. Build up the prestige of each worker

C. Make each one want to get your favorable attention

D. Learn what your subordinates want to accomplish; help them do it

E. Build their confidence in their performance

F. Let each worker know he can count on you for help.

At all times WAI puts major focus on behavior. With the focus on doing the right thing, customer satisfaction is given a high priority. Customer needs are met. Customer complaints are taken very seriously. With mistakes quickly acknowledged, problems are promptly resolved, and everybody moves ahead together.

"We correct the performance, not the worker. We try never to embarrass the person, and we realize that often the most blatant forms of wrong action may be unintentional. Mistakes are treated as correctable misunderstandings. The thrust is to be helpful, impartial and not critical," says Callis.

Wetherill's *Management Techniques for Foremen* outlines a five-step technique for handling problems:

Step 1 - Reduce any problem to a specific question

Step 2 - Improve the wording until it defines your problem exactly

Step 3 - Get a selection of possible answers

Step 4 - Choose the practical ideas that you intend to use

Step 5 - Weave them into a specific plan of action.

At WAI, employees are trained to avoid making critical judgments of people, whether customers, suppliers or coworkers, which causes them to hold grudges that only hurt. Department heads try to distinguish between intentional problems (consistent lateness) and unintentional problems (persons with short fuses who blow up). Wetherill taught that everybody has the capacity to change; people just have to be shown how.

In daily activities at WAI, wrong action calls attention to itself by the wrong results it gets. Right action can replace wrong action with corresponding right results. Threats therefore are unnecessary. Misunderstandings are never held against people, everybody is treated with dignity, and the reality of right results makes the lasting impression.

In business and social life, people ordinarily are told to benchmark against other companies and other people. At WAI, employees benchmark against the Right-Action Ethic. This is highly recommended to everybody. It keeps companies and individuals reaching for top-quality performance in all areas rather than being satisfied with "good enough." To benchmark against right action also enables a person not to take himself too seriously so that he can approach life and business with a sense of humor.

The net result of right thinking, good nurturing and cooperation at WAI is that interpersonal stress within the company is almost nonexistent and severe illnesses are few.

"When the force of right action that reflects the functioning of the universe is followed," says Wetherill, "people are in harmony with nature, with one another and within themselves." The Right-Action Ethic provides a unifying force for all who adopt it. It makes strangers into friends, the frightened into the confident, the weak into the strong; and a true kinship among all members of the human family is born.

That is the success story of Wetherill Associates, Inc.

It can be any company's success story.

It can be your personal success story.

Postscript

Very often the principals of successful companies are asked questions such as: What advice would you pass on to someone else? To whom do you credit your success? Do you feel that you have a mission in life? And so on.

Those questions pose no difficulty at Wetherill Associates, Inc. The answers are given on every page of this book: ***Think, say and do what is right; refuse to think, say and do what is wrong.***

In order to do that, there is one requirement that has to be met, and it is crucial: ***It must be your intent in life to do the right thing at all times as best you can.*** When you find you can't, look for your intent to do or be something other than to be right. Don't make it your primary goal to succeed; to be a leader; to make money; to be popular and well-liked; to be a good boss, worker, spouse, parent; to help your fellowman; or even to save the world for future generations.

The simple intent to do what is right in every situation of life will give you all of those things and more.

The purpose of this book is to share with you the information given to us by Mr. Wetherill so that you can discover why and how effective leadership is found in the unfolding reality of life when it is your intent to do what is right.

The change that people desire on America's social and political scene will not be found by exchanging one person's ideas on how to rescue the country and put people back to work for another person's ideas. The genuine change can come only when there are enough persons with the intent and courage to align themselves with the forces that run the universe, including the force of right. The invisible moral force becomes visible in the results we get: Only right action gets right results; only wrong action gets wrong results.

When we align ourselves with right action, it gives us the kind of leadership that will put America on the right track and take her into the 21st century with true liberty and justice for all.

For more information about other books by Mr. Wetherill or to discuss the Right-Action Ethic, please call: 1-800-992-9124 weekdays between 10 a.m. and 5 p.m. (Eastern time).

Responses From the Business Community

In reference to your "Quality Assurance Manual," I carefully read it after the visit of your kind gentlemen Miles Varner (EXPORT) and David Haugen (MARKETING) to our factory and our city. I found it absolutely GREAT!!!!! Believe me; this is the first time I have (ever had) the pleasure of reading such a constructive, humble, easy and (yet) deep publication written by an important and famous Company like Yours! For these reasons, you surely have deserved your tremendous success and (I) sincerely hope your future will always (get) better as Mr. Richard W. Wetherill was worth being a leader, a teacher, a friend, (to follow) even though I never met him. While I am only 26...his concepts and words (are) so simple that (they) should be taught at school to children and at home to our sons.

Luciano Amodio
FARO Elettromeccanica anc
Lazzaro (BO) ITALY

Our opinion for a long time has been that WAI might dominate the industry of the future, and after attending your technical seminar in Memphis, we are sure. The service is excellent, the employees are always friendly and helpful, and the products are good and competitively priced.

Ed & Helen Pauley
PAULEY MAINTENANCE
Calico Rock, AR

* * *

I want to thank you for helping me find a better way to look at life. Since I started working with WAI three years ago I have become a better person and a happier employee. I feel I can make a difference in the world by doing what is right. I no longer feel I have to bang my head against the door—I can now open it up and walk through. I am always looking for more input!!!!! Thanks again.

Kimberly Laney
Customer Service
WAI
Royersford, PA

Thank you very much for your letter with the booklet titled "Quality Assurance Manual." We were impressed, going through the booklet, not only at the achievements WAI enjoyed these last 10 years but also at HOW it had to be so successful for WAI in such a competitive industry.

Ben Lee, President
SIMMONS INTERNATIONAL
Seoul, Korea

* * *

I have read the Quality Assurance Manual twice on airline trips and have shared the manual with some factory people in Hong Kong and Korea. I am very excited and realize (that) not only will the application of the QAM resolve my quality problems, but all my labor problems will be resolved by applying the same principles.

The foreman and workers had all positive responses to the principles when I translated the QAM to them in Chinese.

(I have sent Copies to my factory directors in Hong Kong, Macao, China and Korea.)

Kevin Chow
PREMIER BEARING & EQUIPMENT LTD.
Hong Kong

Just finished reading your 32-page Quality Assurance Manual. This is really fantastic. I even photocopied your manual so all our supervisors and managers could have their own personal copies. I am sure much work and effort went into producing this manual; as everything WAI comes out with.

Gary Braut
PRECISION BEARING CO.
Hong Kong

* * *

I used to be a high-tech executive in R & D who applied a lot of leadership, a lot of professional learning and a lot of intelligence to business and technical problems. I was frustrated and depressed most of the time.

But then I encountered Wetherill's teachings and learned that elementary honesty is worth legions of leaders, libraries of learning and all the intelligence anyone needs. I found my horizons were limited both by overt and subtle dishonesties I did not see or was unwilling to recognize. I even thought many of my failures were successes! I now know that without honesty, right action is not possible: and without right action, perfect results are not possible.

Perfect results are results that make everyone involved a winner, not just me and my career.

Ed Busch, Director of Engineering
WAI
Royersford, PA

It is obvious to see that WAI knows their business and the entire industry as well. The right management philosophies have been emphasized, and the people feel good about themselves, their work and the company. All this spells success which is evidenced by the .tremendous sales growth you have experienced in the past and will continue to enjoy in the future.

Bob Tracy, Vice President of Operations
AMERICAN CARBON INDUSTRIES
Steubenville, OH

About Mr. Wetherill

Richard W. Wetherill was born in Old Bridge, New Jersey on August 3, 1906, the son of Richard Wayne Wetherill, a civil engineer, and Mary Roberts Wetherill, a schoolteacher. From 1912 to 1928 he attended public schools in the Philadelphia area, and Antioch College in Ohio.

At the age of 23, he embarked on a teaching career and began giving evening classes on Public Speaking and Creative Thinking at the Poor Richard Club in Philadelphia and at YMCA's in Atlantic City, Trenton, Chester and Philadelphia. Early on he was committed to a business life that was to be marked by the highest ethical principles. From 1929 to 1940, he continued his motivational management classes within the business and professional communities in and around the Delaware Valley.

In 1928 he married a local Philadelphia girl, Lou B. Davis. They were together for 61 years until his death in 1989. They had no children.

From 1941 to 1945 he worked for the Edward G. Budd Manufacturing Company while simultaneously publishing his newsletter, *The Creative Thinker,* Volumes 1 and 2 which was issued in 1941 and 1942 until the paper shortage of World War II forced its interruption.

While at the Budd Company, Mr. Wetherill became their Training Executive and introduced the Wetherill Management Seminar that he had developed in the 1930's.

During his years with Budd, he compiled and wrote the first comprehensive book on foremanship under the title, *Management Techniques for Foremen,* along with a Leader's Guide for teaching foremen the principles outlined in the Foremanship book. The books were published by National Foremen's Institute in 1945. National Foremen's Institute also published other material by Wetherill on how to train assistants and similar management topics.

In 1946, Mr. Wetherill resigned from the

Budd company and became a management consultant so that he could work with smaller corporations and help them grow—which they all did.

For the next 13 years the Weidemann Machine Company used his consulting services, during which time the company grew steadily. During his career as a management consultant, he also wrote three books under the general title, *The Dynamics of Human Relations.* Each was a "how to" book: *How To Succeed with People, How To Get Your Ideas Across,* and *How To Get Leadership and Influence.* The three books were published on the same day in 1949 by D. Van Nostrand Co., New York and Toronto. They were placed in U.S. Military Libraries all over the world.

In January 1952 Wetherill published the first book outlining his behavioral study which he called humanetics. The book was titled *Tower of Babel,* and later in the year, his second book on humanetics, *Truth Is Power,* was published. The Right-Action Ethic grew out of the humanetics study.

In 1954, Mr. Wetherill delivered a number of lectures on management principles for the

Cadillac Motor Car Division of General Motors Corporation, and in 1958, he conducted a week-long series of lectures for the Plant Management Training Division of the General Motors Institute in Flint, Michigan.

In 1958, Mr. Wetherill retired from his career as management consultant to devote himself full time to a growing number of people studying the Right-Action Ethic, who were enriching their lives with their study.

In 1959 he resumed publication of *The Creative Thinker,* and by 1981, he had published Volumes 3 through 21 as well as a score of books for use by members of the Behavioral Study Group.

In 1978, 34 of his trainees formed the company, Wetherill Associates, Inc. (WAI), and until his death in 1989, he continued to meet with them and present training in the Right-Action Ethic for management and leadership in business and in private life.

Books By Richard W. Wetherill

- *Management Techniques for Foremen. Leader's Guide*
  Connecticut: National Foremen's Institute, 1946.
- *The Dynamics of Human Relations.* 3 Volumes. "How To Succeed with People." "How To Put Your Ideas Across." "How To Get Leadership and Influence."
  New York: D. Van Nostrand Company, Inc., 1949.
- *Tower of Babel*
  Wynnewood, PA: 1952.
- *Truth is Power*
  Wynnewood, PA: 1952.

The following books are available exclusively from

The Alpha Publishing House
PO Box 255
Royersford • PA 19468
1-800-992-9124

- *Right Is Might*
  Royersford, PA: Humanetics Fellowship, 1991.
- *How To Solve Problems and Prevent Trouble*
  Royersford, PA: Humanetics Fellowship, 1991.
- *Dictionary of Typical Command Phrases*
  Royersford, PA: Humanetics Fellowship, 1992.
- *Suppose We Let Civilization Begin*
  Royersford, PA: Humanetics Fellowship, 1991.